SATs Pr in English

AGE 11

Rhona Whiteford and Jim Fitzsimmons
Illustrated by John Eastwood

The National Curriculum for England and Wales requires all 11 year-olds to be tested in the subjects of English, Mathematics and Science. These tests are called SATs (Standard Assessment Tasks), and are completed during the normal school day. Their purpose is to give schools information about what children are achieving compared to others of the same age, and to highlight areas where help is needed. This book will help you to prepare your child for the SATs in English. Although the SATs are taken at age 11, this book may be used for practice throughout Year 6.

How to help your child

a Working together
If you work through each test with your child, you may discover areas where extra practice is needed. You can provide this by choosing some interesting books and poems, and basing further questions on these.

b Test conditions
The SATs tests are timed at this stage, so you can use this book to prepare your child for real test conditions. Encourage them to work independently, with good concentration and as quickly as possible.

They should do all the tests in each section (for example, Reading) in order, and one at a time.

- Keep sessions short and frequent, perhaps one test per day.
- Make sure you and your child are relaxed and have a quiet place in which to work.
- Avoid putting your child under pressure.
- Build your child's confidence by offering plenty of praise and encouragement.

Hodder Children's Books

The only home learning programme supported by the NCPTA

Reading
COMPREHENSION: FICTION

TEST 1

This extract is from a book called *The Lion, the Witch and the Wardrobe* by C. S. Lewis. A boy called Edmund has gone out into the snows of the magic land of Narnia in search of the White Witch's House. He has already met her and is half under her spell, although he has been warned about her power by the kindly Beavers. He leaves his brother and two sisters and goes out alone.

So he turned up his collar and shuffled across the top of the dam (luckily it wasn't so slippery since the snow had fallen) to the far side of the river.

It was pretty bad when he reached the far side. It was growing darker every minute and what with that and the snowflakes swirling all round him he could hardly see three feet ahead. And then too there was no road. He kept slipping into deep drifts of snow, and skidding on frozen puddles, and tripping over fallen tree-trunks, and sliding down steep banks, and barking his shins against rocks, till he was wet and cold and bruised all over. The silence and the loneliness were dreadful. In fact I really think he might have given up the whole plan and gone back and owned up and made friends with the others, if he hadn't happened to say to himself, "When I'm King of Narnia the first thing I shall do will be to make some decent roads." And of course that set him off thinking about being a

King and all the other things he would do and this cheered him up a good deal.

He would never have found his way if the moon hadn't come out by the time he got to the other river. Even as it was, he got wet through for he had to stoop under branches and great loads of snow came sliding off on to his back. And every time this happened he thought more and more how he hated Peter – just as if all this had been Peter's fault.

But at last he came to a part where it was more level and the valley opened out. And there, on the other side of the river, quite close to him, in the middle of a little plain between two hills, he saw what must be the White Witch's House. And the moon was shing brighter than ever. The House was really a small castle. It seemed to be all towers; little towers with long pointed spires on them, sharp as needles. They looked like huge dunce's caps or sorcerer's caps. And they shone in the moonlight and their long shadows looked strange on the snow. Edmund began to be afraid of the House.

But it was too late to think about turning back now. He crossed the river on the ice and walked up to the House. There was nothing stirring; not the slightest sound anywhere. Even his own feet made no noise on the deep newly fallen snow. He walked on and on, past corner after corner of the House, and past turret after turret to find the door. He had to go right round to the far side before he found it. It was a huge arch but the great iron gates stood wide open.

Edmund crept up to the arch and looked inside into the courtyard, and there he saw a sight that nearly made his heart stop beating. Just inside the gate, with the moonlight shining on it, stood an enormous lion crouched as if it was ready to spring. And Edmund stood in the shadow of the arch, afraid to go on and afraid to go back, with his knees knocking together.

Then at last he began to wonder why the lion was standing so still – for it hadn't moved one inch since he first set eyes on it. Edmund remembered what the others had said about the White Witch turning people into stone. Perhaps this was only a stone lion. And as soon as he had thought of that he noticed that the lion's back and the top of its head were covered with snow. Of

TEST I   **COMPREHENSION: FICTION**

course it must be only a statue! No living animal would have let itself get covered with snow. Then very slowly and with his heart beating as if it would burst, Edmund ventured to go up to the lion. Even now he hardly dared to touch it, but at last he put out his hand, very quickly, and did. It was cold stone. He had been frightened of a mere statue!

The relief which Edmund felt was so great that in spite of the cold he suddenly got warm all over right down to his toes, and at the same time there came into his head what seemed a perfectly lovely idea. "Probably," he thought, "this is the great Lion Aslan that they were all talking about. She's caught him already and turned him into stone. So *that's* the end of all their fine ideas about him! Pooh! Who's afraid of Aslan?"

And he stood there gloating over the stone lion, and presently he did something very silly and childish. He took a stump of lead pencil out of his pocket and scribbled a moustache on the lion's upper lip and then a pair of spectacles on its eyes. Then he said, "Yah! Silly old Aslan! How do you like being a stone? You thought yourself mighty fine, didn't you?" But in spite of the scribbles on it the face of the great stone beast still looked so terrible, and sad, and noble, staring up in the moonlight, that Edmund didn't really get any fun out of jeering at it. He turned away and began to cross the courtyard.

As he got into the middle of it he saw that there were dozens of statues all about — standing here and there rather as the pieces stand on a chess-board when it is half-way through the game. There were stone satyrs, and stone wolves,

COMPREHENSION: FICTION   TEST 1

and bears and foxes and cat-a-mountains of stone. There were lovely stone shapes that looked like women but who were really the spirits of trees. There was the great shape of a centaur and a winged horse and a long lithe creature that Edmund took to be a dragon. They all looked so strange standing there perfectly life-like and also perfectly still, in the bright cold moonlight, that it was eerie work crossing the courtyard.

He now saw that there was a dim light showing from a doorway on the far side of the courtyard. He went to it, there was a flight of stone steps going up to an open door. Edmund went up them. Across the threshold lay a great wolf.

"It's all right, it's all right," he kept saying to himself; "it's only a stone wolf. It can't hurt me," and he raised his leg to step over it. Instantly the huge creature rose, with all the hair bristling along its back, opened a great, red mouth and said in a growling voice:

"Who's there? Who's there? Stand still, stranger, and tell me who you are."

"If you please, sir," said Edmund, trembling so that he could hardly speak, "my name is Edmund, and I'm the Son of Adam that Her Majesty met in the wood the other day and I've come to bring her the news that my brother and sisters are now in Narnia – quite close, in the Beavers' house. She – she wanted to see them."

"I will tell Her Majesty," said the Wolf. "Meanwhile, stand still on the threshold, as you value your life." Then it vanished into the house.

Edmund stood and waited, his fingers aching with cold and his heart pounding in his chest, and presently the grey wolf, Maugrim, the Chief of the Witch's Secret Police, came bounding back and said, "Come in! Come in! Fortunate favourite of the Queen – or else not so fortunate."

5

TEST 1   COMPREHENSION: FICTION

And Edmund went in, taking great care not to tread on the Wolf's paws.

He found himself in a long gloomy hall with many pillars, full, as the courtyard had been, of statues. The one nearest the door was a little faun with a very sad expression on its face, and Edmund couldn't help wondering if this might be Lucy's friend. The only light came from a single lamp and close beside this sat the White Witch.

"I'm come, your Majesty," said Edmund, rushing eagerly forward.

"How dare you come alone?" said the Witch in a terrible voice. "Did I not tell you to bring the others with you?"

"Please, your Majesty," said Edmund, "I've done the best I can. I've brought them quite close. They're in the little house on top of the dam just up the river – with Mr. and Mrs. Beaver."

A slow cruel smile came over the Witch's face.

"Is this all your news?" she asked.

"No, your Majesty," said Edmund, and proceeded to tell her all he had heard before leaving the Beavers' house.

"What! Aslan?" cried the Queen, "Aslan! Is this true? If I find you have lied to me –"

"Please, I'm only repeating what they said," stammered Edmund.

But the Queen, who was no longer attending to him, clapped her hands. Instantly the same dwarf whom Edmund had seen with her before appeared.

"Make ready our sledge," ordered the Witch, "and use the harness without bells."

Abridged from *The Lion, the Witch and the Wardrobe* by C.S. Lewis

COMPREHENSION: FICTION   TEST 1

■ QUESTIONS ■

The story

1 What was the weather like?

   raining ☐   dark and snowy ☐   light and warm ☐

2 Edmund was

   looking through a window ☐   on a journey ☐   in a cave ☐

3 What was shining on the snow?

   the sun ☐   a full moon ☐   a light ☐

4 When he found the White Witch's House, Edmund saw that it was really

   a big building ☐   a small castle ☐   white with snow ☐

5 What did Edmund see just inside the open gates of the huge arch?

   _____

6 When he saw that all the figures were made of stone, who did he think the stone lion was?

   the Witch herself ☐   no one special ☐   Aslan ☐

7 When Edmund crossed the courtyard he saw a great wolf lying across the threshold of the open door. Why did he get a shock when he tried to pass it?

   _____

   _____

8 Who did he meet next? _____

9 What news did Edmund tell the White Witch?

   all he had heard before leaving the Beavers' house ☐

   all about Aslan's plans ☐   all about his own plans ☐

7

TEST 1　　　COMPREHENSION: FICTION

■ QUESTIONS ■

The characters

10 Edmund thought he was very important and would soon be made even more important. What did he say he would become?

_____

11 What did Edmund do to the statue of the lion, and why?

_____

_____

12 – 14 Describe three things that were frightening about the wolf.

_____

_____

_____

15 – 16 Which two words might describe the Witch?

_____

_____

8

COMPREHENSION: FICTION — TEST I

■ QUESTIONS ■

The style

17 – 18 The writer describes in detail two things that make Edmund's journey to the Witch's House so hard. What are they?

_____

_____

19 – 21 The writer takes Edmund to three different places. In one he is quite bold, in the second he is frightened and in the third he is shocked because he doesn't find what he expects. What are these places?

_____

_____

_____

22 – 24 Which three adjectives (describing words) does the writer use most often to describe the statues?

_____

_____

TEST 1 COMPREHENSION: FICTION

■ QUESTIONS ■

Your opinion

25 – 26 Did you enjoy reading this extract?   yes ☐   no ☐

Give reasons for your answer, describing what you did or did not like about the extract.

_____

_____

27 – 28 What do you think made Edmund keep on going although his journey across country was very hard?

_____

29 – 30 Do you think Edmund was frightened when he got to the Witch's House? If so, what do you think it was that frightened him?

_____

31 – 32 Would you like to have been on this adventure instead of Edmund? Give a reason for your answer.

_____

_____

33 – 34 Do you think the cold, the snow and the silence are important in this part of Edmund's adventure? Give a reason for your answer.

_____

_____

TEST 2

Pirate Story

Three of us afloat in the meadow by the swing,
Three of us aboard in the basket on the lea,
Winds are in the air, they are blowing in the spring,
And waves are on the meadow like the waves there are at sea.

Where shall we adventure, today that we're afloat,
Wary of the weather and steering by a star?
Shall it be to Africa, a-steering of the boat,
To Providence, or Babylon, or off to Malabar?

Hi! but here's a squadron a-rowing on the sea –
Cattle on the meadow a-charging with a roar!
Quick and we'll escape them, they're mad as they can be,
The wicket is the harbour and the garden is the shore.

by Robert Louis Stevenson

TEST 2　　　　　　　COMPREHENSION: FICTION

■ **QUESTIONS** ■

1　Who do you think is speaking in this poem?

_____

2　What makes you think this?

_____

3　What is the imaginary boat?
　　a box ☐　　a basket ☐　　an old log ☐

4　What time of year is it? _____

5　The **waves on the meadow** are
　　a flood of water from a stream ☐
　　long grasses that are moving in the wind ☐　　drifts of snow ☐

6　**Wary of the weather** means
　　watchful in case the weather changes ☐
　　enjoying the weather ☐　　ignoring the weather ☐

7　How do you know that the child is pretending that it is night-time?

_____

8　What is the **squadron a-rowing on the sea**?

_____

9 – 10　What did the "sailors" do when the cows charged?

_____

COMPREHENSION: NON-FICTION

TEST 3

Lifesavers of the RNLI

DANGER!
The oceans and seas are always moving because of the tides and the weather. We know when the tides are going to change, but the weather around the British Isles can change suddenly and dramatically. Anyone near or on the seas around our coasts can find themselves in great danger in a matter of minutes. Many people have lost their lives in terrible storms and accidents at sea.

HELP AT LAST
In 1824, the RNLI (Royal National Lifeboat Institution) was formed to help people in trouble at sea.

One story in particular caught the public's attention. On a stormy night in 1838, Grace Darling and her father saved the lives of nine men, women and children in a daring rescue from the wild seas of the Farne Islands.

In 1851 there was a national competition for a lifeboat design. The winner designed a self-righting lifeboat, and this idea was used for the next 50 years. This important invention kept the lifeboat crews safer. Steam was being used to power the new factories, and in 1890 the first steam-powered lifeboat was launched.

SAVING LIVES

Since 1869 the RNLI has saved the lives of more than 120,000 people. In 1990 alone, nearly 5,000 calls for help were answered. Because we live in a group of islands, nowhere in Britain is more than 75 miles from the sea. At this very moment, a lifeboat may be out on a rescue mission.

BRAVE CREWS

Lifeboats are crewed by volunteers: men and women who are good sailors and brave enough to risk their lives for others but who get no payment for this service. They all have other jobs, but they are on call at any time of the day or night. They can be called out in any weather to face any kind of danger. But the running of Britain's 210 lifeboat stations needs teams of people. There are volunteers who run the stations, maintain the boats and raise funds locally – most of the RNLI's funding comes from the public. Coastguards and the land-based emergency services are sometimes needed to help with rescues.

FAST RESPONSE

Lifeboat design has advanced tremendously in the last hundred years, and there is a lifeboat suitable for every kind of rescue. There are 13 different "classes", all of which have the fastest engines available. Some are moored afloat, and some need to be launched down a slipway.

In 1963 the first inflatable was used. These are popular for inshore rescue, especially in shallow waters. The children's television programme "Blue Peter" has organised many appeals and has bought several inflatable boats for the RNLI.

YOU CAN HELP

If you want to learn more about the work of the RNLI you can join the fundraising children's club "Stormforce". New members of the club receive an exciting pack containing a copy of *Stormforce News*, a membership badge, a certificate and some posters.

Write to:
> Stormforce HQ
> RNLI
> West Quay Road
> Poole
> Dorset BH15 1HZ

IT COULD BE YOU!

The RNLI rescues people in many different situations. For example, a fishing boat may capsize in a storm, a sailing yacht may lose a mast in a high wind, a child's dinghy may be blown out of its depth, or a lone sailor may be taken ill aboard his boat. Danger on the sea comes in many forms, but the RNLI is always ready, always fast and always brave. Remember, one of *your* family could be that person in need.

TEST 3   COMPREHENSION: NON-FICTION

■ QUESTIONS ■

1 The oceans and seas of the world are always
   moving ☐   still ☐   flat ☐

2 Many people have lost their lives in
   lifeboats ☐   terrible storms and accidents at sea ☐

3 The RNLI was formed   to help people in trouble at sea ☐
   to collect money for boats ☐   to help the crews ☐

4 Where does the RNLI get most of its money from?
   _____

5 A **volunteer** crew member is someone who is
   _____

6 – 7   Which other services sometimes help with rescues?
   _____

8 Which type of boat is suitable for inshore rescue in shallow waters?
   _____

9 Which club could you join to find out more about the RNLI?
   _____

10 If you join "Stormforce", what will you receive?
   _____
   _____
   _____

11 Name one dangerous situation at sea which may result in people needing to be rescued.
   _____

16

COMPREHENSION: NON-FICTION   TEST 4

TEST 4

Is this the beast of Craigside?

The farming community around Craigside Castle is becoming increasingly alarmed. Eight sheep have been killed and two seriously injured during the last two weeks.

There have been six sightings of a large creature in the area during this time. Jamie Argyll saw it last Monday evening at about 7 o'clock.

"It was lurking in the long bracken behind the old barn at my farm, but it ran off as I approached," said Jamie.

Fiona McLeod said, "I've never seen anything like it! When it growled, it was louder than a crack of thunder!"

Fiona's sister added, "I think it must have escaped from a zoo."

After finding two of his best young sheep slaughtered, Sandy McNiven said, "The creature that did this must have claws like daggers."

The police have organised a search for the creature, and a reward of £500 has been offered for any information that leads to its capture.

Local wildlife ranger Angus McTigue said, "From what we have got so far, I think the creature could turn out to be a large wildcat."

MA

For th
Marti
East

17

TEST 4   COMPREHENSION: NON-FICTION

THE WILDCAT

The Latin name for the wildcat is *felis silvestris*. The name for the Scottish subspecies is *felis silvestris Grampia*. The Scottish wildcat produces two litters of kittens a year in May and August, and occasionally a third litter in December or January.

Most wildcats have striped tabby coats, but sometimes they interbreed with domestic cats so there can be great variations. Descendants of domestic cats which have turned wild may increase considerably in size, and become as fierce as the true wildcat.

Wildcats are meat eaters, and their diet consists of rats, mice, rabbits and small birds. They prefer to live and hunt alone (except during the breeding season).

■ QUESTIONS ■

1 – 8   From the report on page 17, select four sentences which are presented as facts and four sentences which are presented as the opinions of characters.

Facts

_____

_____

_____

_____

COMPREHENSION: NON-FICTION

TEST 4

_____
_____
_____
_____

Opinions

_____
_____
_____
_____
_____
_____
_____
_____

These questions are about the information on page 18.

9 What colour is a wildcat's coat? _____

10 How many litters of kittens does a wildcat have each year?
_____

11 The Latin name for the Scottish wildcat is

felis silvestris ☐   *felis domesticus* ☐   *felis silvestris Grampia* ☐

12 What do wildcats prey on?
_____

19

TEST 5

WELCOME TO CRAIGSIDE CASTLE

CASTLE OF THE YEAR 1996

Situated on the A523, 1.5 miles west of Seacombe

Take the No.7 bus from Seacombe to Muckleford

Open all year round except Christmas Day
Castle 12.00 noon to 5.00 p.m.
Gardens 1.00 a.m. to 6.00 p.m.
Guided tours every half-hour from 12.00 noon
Last admission 4.00 p.m.

ADMISSION
Castle and gardens   Adult £3.00   Child £1.50
Gardens only   Adult £1.00   Child £0.50

See the falcons fly!
2.00 p.m. and 3.00 p.m.

- Mini-Golf Course
- Gift Shop
- Giant Maze
- Adventure Playground
- Nature Trail
- Dungeon Tea Rooms

Special Events This Year

CRAFT FAIR June 6th and 7th   VINTAGE CAR RALLY August 15th - 18th

COMPREHENSION: NON-FICTION TEST 5

■ QUESTIONS ■

1 For how many hours each day is the castle open? _____

2 Where is the castle situated?
   _____

3 At which times do the falcons fly?
   _____

4 Which award did the castle win?
   _____

5 How much does it cost to visit the castle and the gardens?

   Adult _____   Child _____

6 – 9 List four outdoor attractions at Craigside Castle.
   _____   _____
   _____   _____

10 Which bus do you take from Seacombe to get to the castle?

   No.4 ☐   No.9 ☐   No.5 ☐   No.7 ☐   No.6 ☐

11 Which special events are advertised?
   _____

12 At which time is the last admission to the castle?

   2.00 p.m. ☐   6.00 p.m. ☐   3.00 p.m. ☐   4.00 p.m. ☐

13 On which day is the castle closed?
   _____

Writing

STORY WRITING

TEST 6

Choose one of the ideas below as a starting point for writing a story. Use the boxes on page 23 to note down some of your ideas for the story.
Spend 10–15 minutes on Test 6 (planning your story) and then move on to Test 7 (writing your story).

A   You are visiting a castle where you get lost in a maze of corridors. As you search for a way out, you accidentally lean against a carved panel which swings open to reveal a secret passage. Write a story about what happens.

B   You are listening to the local radio station when suddenly the programme is interrupted by an SOS message. A storm is raging and some people on a yacht are in danger of drowning. You just have time to scribble details of their position before your radio aerial is hit by the storm. Write a story about what you do next.

C   You are a keen nature lover. One day, while visiting your local beauty spot, you overhear a conversation between two officials discussing plans for a new factory to be built there. It is the only woodland in the area. Write a story about what you do next and whose help you seek.

STORY WRITING — TESTS 6/7

■ STORY PLANNING ■

Title
_____

1 – 2 Setting (Where and when does it happen?)
_____
_____

3 – 4 Characters (Who are they? What are they like?)
_____
_____

5 – 6 How does the story begin?
_____
_____

7 – 8 What is the main event?
_____
_____

9 – 10 How does the story end?
_____
_____

■ STORY WRITING ■

TEST 7

1 – 10 Now write your story on a sheet of paper.

LETTER WRITING

TEST 8

Choose one of the ideas below as a starting point for writing a letter. Use the boxes on page 25 to make notes about what you want to say in your letter. Spend 5–10 minutes on Test 8 (planning your letter) and then move on to Test 9 (writing your letter).

A You are on an adventure holiday, and you write a letter home telling of all the exciting things you have done since you arrived.

B One of your favourite children's television programmes is about to be taken off the air. The presenter has invited children to write to the television company to ask for the show to be saved. Write a letter, giving as many reasons as you can for the programme to continue.

C You have a penfriend who lives in another country. Write a letter inviting them to stay with you for a holiday. Tell them about all the things you will do and the exciting places you will visit. Draw on your own real experiences.

D Your favourite band is due to appear at the local theatre, and there is a competition to win four free tickets and the chance to go backstage. All you have to do is to write a letter to the manager of the theatre, saying why you like the band and why you would like to meet them, and listing three questions you would like to ask them.

LETTER WRITING   TESTS 8/9

■ **LETTER PLANNING** ■

1 – 2   Who will you address the letter to?
_____

3 – 5   How will the letter begin?
_____
_____

6 – 8   What do you want to say in your letter? Make some notes here.
_____
_____
_____
_____
_____
_____

9 – 10 How will you end your letter?
_____
_____

■ **LETTER WRITING** ■

TEST 9

1 – 10 Now write your letter on a sheet of paper.

SPELLING

TEST 10

1 – 55   Listen carefully the first time this story is read to you. As it is read for the second time, fill in the missing words, making sure you spell them correctly.

The Golden Eagle

"I've got a golden eagle. I keep it _____ home. I have to feed it raw meat or it _____ upset!" Davy looked smug as he told Mike his latest _____. "I hold it on my fist and feed it lumps of _____," he added, holding his arm outstretched to _____ his friend.

Mike looked at him thoughtfully. He wasn't _____ whether to believe Davy. He always came up with good _____, but that's just what they were – stories, from his _____ imagination. "What's it like, then?" he _____ suspiciously.

This was just what Davy had been hoping for. "Well, it's got _____ talons, and each of its feet is as big as my _____. Its legs are feathered but its feet are _____ of yellow and scaly like a dinosaur _____ have had. Its feathers are dark _____ all over except for a golden tinge to its head. Like the sun on top of a _____." Davy smiled as he described it, and his _____ became dreamy.

"What's its _____ like? Has it got teeth as big as your fingers?" Mike _____, but Davy was serious.

"Birds don't have teeth, silly. Its beak is huge — _____ and curved, and so sharp it can tear raw meat from the _____. Wait until you see it."

Mike _____ to look scared. "Well, I hope my bones are safe. Aren't those birds dangerous or _____?" he asked, _____ believing Davy now.

TEST 10 — SPELLING

"You're too skinny!" laughed Davy. "They're very _____ to their prey. Look out if you're a _____, a hare, a grouse or even a little _____."

Mike laughed. "My Mum says I'm a little lamb." He pursed his lips and _____ to look lamb-like. He wondered how big the eagle _____. Could it fit in a shed, or did it need a huge _____ like the ones at the bird rescue place they had visited with their _____?

Davy went on describing the golden eagle. It has a wingspan of two metres, and _____ its eyrie, which is the name of its nest, out of piles of _____ and twigs. Not too comfy for the nestlings, _____ Mike. Eagles build their eyries about 500 metres above sea level on _____ in Scotland. The pair (the _____ and the female) repair their nest in November and December. Mike was _____ that it must be quite snowy in the Highlands.

"They _____ a clutch of eggs in March or April," Davy went on knowledgeably. He _____ as if he'd swallowed an encyclopaedia. "There are

_____ only two eggs, white with red-brown markings."

Davy had _____ Mike's interest now, and he looked at his _____ with respect. "Well, I'd certainly like to see your _____ eagle. How did you get it? I thought they were very _____."

Davy drew him down the garden path towards the shed. "_____ are, and my Dad paid a lot for this one. It's 50 years old," he said, opening the door to the _____.

Mike held his _____. Would it attack him? He winced in case it _____ too loudly.

"Well, what do you think? Isn't it a _____?" breathed Davy, with a _____ sweep of his arm in the direction of his _____ workbench. A fierce eye stared at _____ from the gloom, and Mike held his _____.

"Why _____ it move?" he whispered from _____ Davy's back.

"Stuffed birds don't move ..." Davy _____ resist a smirk.

HANDWRITING

TEST 11

The Eagle

He clasps the crag with crooked hands;
Close to the sun in lonely lands,
Ringed with the azure world, he stands.

The wrinkled sea beneath him crawls;
He watches from his mountain walls,
And like a thunderbolt he falls.

by Alfred Lord Tennyson

Copy this poem carefully, in your best handwriting.

ANSWERS

Test 1
1. dark and snowy
2. on a journey
3. a full moon
4. a small castle
5. an enormous lion crouched as if it was ready to spring
6. Aslan
7. The wolf was alive, and rose to speak.
8. the White Witch
9. all he had heard before leaving the Beavers' house
10. King of Narnia
11. He drew on its face with a pencil, because he found that it was made of stone and couldn't harm him.
12 – 14 Any of the following:
   it lay across the threshold,
   it was huge,
   all the hair on its back was bristling,
   it opened its great red mouth,
   it had a growling voice,
   it ordered Edmund to stand still,
   it bounded back to him
15 – 16 Any of the following:
   unfriendly, bad-tempered, angry, cruel, suspicious, impatient, threatening, terrible
17 – 18 the weather and the darkness
19 – 21 the countryside, the courtyard and the long, gloomy hall
22 – 24 cold, still, stone
25 – 26 Either answer is valid as long as a good reason is given, and it is written as a complete sentence.
27 – 28 Any of the following:
   the thought of becoming King of Narnia,
   getting his own back on Peter,
   any other answer supported by something in the text
29 – 30 Any of the following:
   the stone lion, the real wolf, the changed manner of the Witch
31 – 32 Any answer is valid as long as a good reason is given, and it is written as a complete sentence.
33 – 34 Any answer is valid as long as a good reason is given, and it is written as a complete sentence.

Test 2
1. A child is speaking.
2. He or she is pretending to be in a ship.
3. a basket
4. spring
5. long grasses that are moving in the wind
6. watchful in case the weather changes
7. He or she talks of steering by a star, which would only be seen at night.
8. cattle on the meadow
9 – 10 They ran through a gate and into the garden.

Test 3
1. moving
2. terrible storms and accidents at sea
3. to help people in trouble at sea
4. the public
5. a good sailor and brave enough to risk their life for others, but who works without pay
6 – 7 coastguards and the land-based emergency services
8. an inflatable
9. "Stormforce"
10. an exciting pack containing a copy of *Stormforce News*, a membership badge, a certificate and some posters
11. Any of the following:
   a fishing boat may capsize in a storm,
   a sailing boat may lose a mast in a high wind,
   a child's dinghy may be blown out of its depth,
   a lone sailor may be taken ill aboard his boat

Test 4
1 – 4 Any of the following:
   Eight sheep have been killed and two seriously injured during the last two weeks.
   There have been six sightings of a large creature in the area during this time.

31

Jamie Argyll saw it last Monday evening at about 7 o'clock.
The police have organised a search for the creature, and a reward of £500 has been offered for any information that leads to its capture.

5 – 8 Any of the following:
When it growled, it was louder than a crack of thunder!
I think it must have escaped from a zoo.
The creature that did this must have claws like daggers.
From what we have got so far, I think the creature could turn out to be a large wildcat.

9   tabby
10 usually two, sometimes three
11 *felis silvestris Grampia*
12 rats, mice, rabbits and small birds

Test 5

1   5 hours
2   on the A523, 1.5 miles west of Seacombe
3   2.00 p.m. and 3.00 p.m.
4   Castle of the Year
5   £3.00 £1.50
6 – 9 Any of the following:
gardens, nature trail, giant maze, adventure playground, mini-golf course
10 No.7
11 a Craft Fair and a Vintage Car Rally
12 4.00 p.m.
13 Christmas Day

Tests 6 – 9 See notes on assessment (inside front cover).

Test 10

1 – 55 at gets news meat show sure stories brilliant asked huge hand sort might brown mountain eyes beak laughed powerful bones pretended something almost dangerous rabbit lamb tried was cage school builds sticks thought mountainsides male thinking lay sounded usually caught friend golden rare They shed breath screeched beauty majestic Dad's them breath doesn't behind couldn't

The first time you read the story, fill the gaps with the words above. Omit them on the second reading, asking your child to write them down. In some cases, alternative answers would be equally acceptable, so encourage intelligent guesses.

Test 11 See notes on assessment (inside front cover).

ISBN 0 340 68070 9

Text © Jim Fitzsimmons and Rhona Whiteford 1997
The Lion, the Witch and the Wardrobe by C.S. Lewis © the Estate of C.S. Lewis 1950. Reproduced by permission of HarperCollins Publishers Ltd.

Illustrations © John Eastwood 1997

The right of Jim Fitzsimmons and Rhona Whiteford to be identified as the authors of this work have been asserted by them in accordance with the Copyright, Design and Patents Act 1988.

First published in Great Britain 1997

10 9 8 7 6 5 4 3

All rights reserved. No part of this publication may be reproduced, stored in a retrieval system, or transmitted, in any form or by any means, without the prior written permission of the publisher, nor be otherwise circulated in any form of binding or cover other than that in which it is published and without a similar condition being imposed on the subsequent purchaser.

Published by
Hodder Children's Books,
a division of Hodder Headline
338 Euston Road, London NW1 3BH

Printed and bound in Great Britain

A CIP record is registered by and held at the British Library.